Coffee Talk with Jesus:

Intimate Chats with the Savior

Barbie Swihart

MyFreshlyBrewedLife.com

Coffee Talk with Jesus: Intimate Chats with the Savior

Copyright © 2013

Barbie Swihart of myfreshlybrewedlife.com.

Unless otherwise indicated, all Scripture quotations are from The Holy Bible, English Standard Version® (ESV®), copyright © 2001 by Crossway, a publishing ministry of Good News Publishers. Used by permission. All rights reserved.

Cover design, editing, Kindle conversion, and CreateSpace conversion was provided by HelpyHelperVAServices.com.

Table of Contents

Introduction: The Invitation

The door is standing wide open. Can you smell the aroma of freshly brewed coffee? There are also assorted juices, lots of fruit, and fresh pastries — all waiting for YOU!

I can hear Him as He beckons me to come, can you? I enter the room and look for an empty seat. I don't like crowds much, so I head for a chair off in the corner. I like to hide sometimes, tucking myself away quietly while I wait. He promises that if I come with an expectant heart, He will speak. And so I wait. With my journal open and pen ready, I take a sip of my freshly brewed coffee and savor the aroma. And I am reminded of how much better the aroma of His fragrance is.

Will you come in and have a seat? He's calling you to come and sit a while. He longs to share His heart with you. In the midst of the quiet and in the middle of the hustle and bustle, He is here, waiting for you. I can hear Him now.

"Come to me, My child, My precious daughter, for I long to share my heart with you today. Will you stop for just a moment and allow yourself to be still so I can talk with you? I have so much to share with

you. I have prepared a place for you, and it is filled with the freshly brewed fragrance of my love. Will you come and sit? Will you come and hear my heart for you today?"

Over the next 31 days, we will embark on a journey together. My prayer is that you will be taken deeper into His love as the fragrance of His aroma surrounds you. These words are meant to be savored slowly. As His words wash over you, my prayer is that the aroma of God's love will fill your heart to overflowing and you will be awakened to a deeper revelation of His love for you.

So grab your coffee or tea. Get your journal and pen ready. Come with an expectant heart. Come just as you are. He is speaking. Are you listening?

Day 1: Come Away With Me

Your mind is racing, and your heart is beating fast. There are so many things to do, so many people wanting your full attention. You struggle, falling under the weight of it. You call out to Me, *"Which way do I go?"*

Your responsibilities seem overwhelming at times. And you cry out, *"Lord, can I just please have a few more hours in my day?"*

I have ordained each day, from the rising of the sun to its setting, to hold the time allotted for you to accomplish all that I've called you to do. *"But, Lord, what is it that you want me to do?"*

I want you to breathe, to inhale My presence. It's okay to rest. I give you permission to slow down and cease from your striving.

Don't be worried by the silence. Just listen for the whisper of My voice. It will come through loud and clear as you come away and rest. Come away with Me and allow Me to speak to your heart.

My beloved speaks and says to me: "Arise, my love, my beautiful one, and come away
(Song of Solomon 2:10)

Reflection

Put on soft worship music. Spend a few moments in prayer and quiet your heart. Now, ask the Lord to show you a picture of a place where it's just you and Him. What does it look like? Notice your surroundings. Write down what you see.

_____

_____

_____

_____

_____

_____

_____

_____

_____

Prayer

Father, I desire to come away with You. Will you take me to that place, God, where it's just You and me? Will you reveal Your love to my heart and reaffirm who it is I am in You? Thank you that You desire to spend intimate moments with me and share Your heart with me.

Day 2: Do You Trust Me?

Now that you are here and I have your full attention, I want you to know that it's okay to let your guard down. I see the walls that you've put up to avoid being hurt. I know that you feel a need to protect yourself. But I want you to know that you can trust me. I will never violate your trust, and I will never force you into relationship. My love for you is patient. As you sit in the corner waiting for me to speak, I am waiting for you to come — fully, completely and without restraint.

Trust me when you cannot see,
for I am the Light in the darkness.

Trust me when you do not understand,
allowing My light to give you wisdom.

Trust me when it's painful,
allowing My light to bring hope and healing.

Will you give me your whole heart — undivided, yielded, and surrendered? Your heart is fragile, yes, but in the palm of My hand, it is made strong. In My hands you are secure and loved, without conditions, and cared for deeply. Trust Me. I will not hurt you.

Reflection

Are there things in your life that have made it hard for you to trust God? What are you afraid of? What do you think will happen if you trust God completely? Will you be honest with God today about your fears?

_____

_____

_____

_____

_____

_____

_____

_____

_____

_____

Prayer

Father, I come to You now, and I surrender my fears of trusting You completely. Will You help me to see You, Jesus? You have been here all along, even in the places of deep hurt and pain. Today I surrender my life into Your hands. Thank You for being a good, loving, and patient Father

Café Coffee Cookies

Adapted from Betty Crocker

Cookies

½ Cup Granulated Sugar

½ Cup Packed Brown Sugar

½ Cup Butter Or Margarine, Softened

1 Egg

1 ½ Cups Gold Medal® All-Purpose Flour

1 Tablespoon Instant Coffee Granules Or Instant Espresso Coffee (Dry)

1 Teaspoon Baking Soda

¼ Teaspoon Salt

½ Cup Chopped Pecans

1 Bag (11.5 Or 12 Oz) Semisweet Chocolate Chips (2 Cups)

Coffee Drizzle

½ Teaspoon Instant Coffee Granules Or Instant Espresso Coffee (Dry)

1 Tablespoon Water

½ Cup Powdered Sugar

Instructions

Heat oven to 350°F. In large bowl, beat granulated and brown sugars, butter and egg with electric mixer on medium speed, or mix with spoon, until creamy. Stir in flour, 1 tablespoon coffee granules, the baking soda and salt. Stir in pecans and chocolate chips.

Drop dough by 1/4 cupful about 2 inches apart onto ungreased large cookie sheet.

Bake 12 to 15 minutes or until golden brown and edges are set. Cool 4 minutes; remove from cookie sheet to wire rack. Cool completely, about 30 minutes.

Meanwhile, in small bowl, dissolve 1/2 teaspoon coffee granules in water. Stir in powdered sugar until smooth and thin enough to drizzle.

Drizzle cooled cookies with Coffee Drizzle

Day 3: I Am a Good Father

My daughter, trust Me when I tell you that I am a good Father. I know you've been searching your entire life for love and acceptance. You do not need to look any longer, for I, Your Heavenly Father, love and accept you just as you are.

My love for you is everlasting. I will never hurt or abandon you. I will never fail you, and I will never take my eyes off of you. Every tear that you've cried I've caught with my hands and placed in a bottle. I am well acquainted with your grief. I've been right beside you, even when you felt all hope was gone.

Cast off the lies that tell you that you are unlovable, unwanted, and worthless. Will you look up today, my precious one, into the eyes of the One who will love you through all eternity?

You are not abandoned.
You are cherished.

You are not tossed aside.
You are treasured.

You are not unwanted
You are chosen.

You are not unlovable.
You are My delight!

Lift your eyes, oh, daughter of God, and begin to walk in your true identity as a chosen, desired, and loved daughter of your perfect, Heavenly Father!

Reflection

Describe your earthly father. What do you love about him? Where do you feel your father came up short? Are there places in your heart that you desire God to heal because of a broken or painful relationship with your father? What happened? How do you feel about it today? How is God, your Heavenly Father, different from your earthly father?

_____

_____

_____

_____

_____

_____

_____

_____

_____

_____

Prayer

Heavenly Father, thank You that You love me. Help me understand that You are a perfect Father – loving, compassionate, and generous in all Your ways. Help me to forgive my earthly father for any hurt and disappointment that he may have caused me. Help me to be a better daughter, by healing me from the inside out so that I reflect Your love.

Day 4: Just Breathe

I am so glad you came to sit and talk with Me today. I can feel your heart expanding in the palm of my hand. Don't forget that I am your Protector. As we take this journey together, I will take your fragile and often overworked heart and allow it to do nothing but grow in my grasp.

There is no need to be fearful of the next step. I can hear you breathing. You've had a long day, and I can feel the weight of it on your shoulders. I do not want you to labor for your next breath. I promise you that no matter how you are feeling right at this moment, I will not allow you to suffocate under the weight of what it is you are carrying.

I know you are tired. I understand that sometimes you feel as if you don't have strength for the journey. It's often hard to put into words what you carry in your heart, isn't it?

Will you do something for me? Will you breathe? Now, I know what you are thinking, *"Lord, I am already breathing otherwise I wouldn't be here."* This is true. But I want to teach you to breathe in a different way. First, I want you to close your eyes.

You may want to put your coffee down, just for a moment. I promise I will let you finish it. Now close your eyes. Next, I want you to take a big, deep breath. And as you inhale, I am filling you with my own breath — the Breath of Life. These deep, cleansing breaths are good for your spirit, soul, and body.

Now I want you to exhale. Go ahead. Blow out all of the stuff that doesn't belong — disappointment, worry, fear of failure, fear that you aren't measuring up, lost hope, unmet expectations. These were never yours to carry in the first place. Remember how I told you that my yoke is easy and my burden is light? How can you breathe properly when you carry the weight of the world on your shoulders?

With every breath you take, I am filling you with peace, joy, and hope. So before you leave today, remember to take several more deep breaths. I want you to feel My presence with you when you leave. Now go ahead and finish your coffee. But promise to come back tomorrow. We have some more work to do.

"For my yoke is easy and my burden is light."
(Matthew 11:30)

Reflection

What burdens are you carrying today? Write them down. What burdens are you ready to let go of? Will you lay them down today? Allow God to take them from you and lighten your load.

_____

_____

_____

_____

_____

_____

_____

_____

_____

_____

Prayer

Father, will You take the burdens from me that have been weighing heavily on my heart? Forgive me for trying to carry them on my own. Father, You said that Your yoke is easy, and Your burden is light. Will You come and lift these burdens from my shoulders, and replace them with peace, hope, and joy? Thank you, Lord, for lightening my load.

Cafe Vienna

*Denise In Bloom. Used with permission.

Ingredients

2/3 Cups Sugar

¼ Cup Powdered Coffee Creamer

½ Cup Instant Coffee Granules

½ Cup Dry Milk

¼ Cup Instant Butterscotch Pudding Mix

1 Teaspoon Cinnamon

Instructions

To a cup of hot water, add 2 teaspoons of the Cafe Vienna mix and stir until dissolved.

Day 5: I See You

What is this talk about hiding in a corner? You say you don't like to be among the crowd, to be seen, but deep down inside, you are longing for someone to see you, to really see you. When you were a child, do you remember playing hide-and-seek? You were always the one seeking after others who were longing to be found, wanting to be seen.

At times you've been misunderstood, left alone, or not included. You feel as if you don't belong. You could be in a room filled with people and still feel as if no one truly sees you. But I see you there, restless in your chair, cradling that cup of warm tea in your hands. Your eyes meet mine and then turn away. You are longing to be seen yet you are afraid to be seen. Why do you fear being accepted for who you really are? My eyes peer deeply into your soul. And what I see is beautiful. What I see is good. What I see deserves to be seen by others.

Whenever you feel alone, I want you to remember that I am the God who sees you.

"She gave this name to the LORD who spoke to her: "You are the God who sees me," for she said, "I have now seen the One who sees me." (Genesis 16:13)

Reflection

Do you feel unseen by others, or are you afraid of being seen? How does it make you feel when others overlook you? What is it that makes you feel unworthy of the delight of others?

_____

_____

_____

_____

_____

_____

_____

_____

_____

_____

Prayer

Father, I admit that I often feel alone and unseen. I would rather hide, far away from the peering eyes of a demanding world because I often feel unworthy of being seen. Will You remind me, Lord, of my worth in You? Will You remind me, Father, that You are the God who sees me? Thank you, Lord, that You delight in me, and that is truly all that matters.

Day 6: Take Off the Labels

There you are! I've been waiting for you to come! You make me smile when you walk into the room. Don't worry about your hair. I know you've had a long day. You don't ever have to clean yourself up to come and chat with me. Remember, I love you just the way you are. Grab your cup of hot cocoa, and let's chat.

Today I want to talk about labels, those that you carry around with you everywhere you go. I can see them. They are all over you. But, My love, these words were never chosen for you. These words do not define you, but you have allowed yourself to be identified by them, at least in your own mind. These invisible untruths have put a hole in your heart so big that filling it with My truth seems overwhelming.

Today I want to help you begin to remove these negative labels and replace them with the truth found in My Love Letter to you.

When you tell yourself that you are not enough,
Don't you realize that you are more than a
conqueror because you love Me
and I have called you?
(Romans 8:37)

When you call yourself ugly,
Don't you realize that you are beautiful in My eyes?
(Song of Solomon 4:7)

When you call yourself weak and ineffective,
Don't you realize that in your weakness I am made
strong? (2 Corinthians 12:9)

When you tell yourself that you are undesirable,
Don't you realize that My desire for you is strong?
(Song of Solomon 7:10)

Do you feel lighter now? We have only just begun. I
want you to go and tuck yourself away in the secret
place. Take My Love Letter with you and look for
truths that will help you break free of the lies that
you've believed about yourself for too long.

I can't wait until we meet again tomorrow!

Reflection

What are some of the negative labels that you have identified with through the years? Write them down. Write down the opposite, positive labels. Ask Jesus to help you to replace the negative labels with the positive ones. Ask Him to help you believe that you are who He says you are.

Prayer

Father, forgive me for allowing myself to believe lies. Will You help me to remove these labels and replace them with what Your Word says about me? Thank you, Lord, for loving me just as I am.

Chocolate Mint Coffee

*Denise In Bloom. Used with permission.

Ingredients

½ Cup Dutch Cocoa

¾ Cup Non-Dairy Creamer

¾ Cup Powdered Sugar

½ Teaspoon Peppermint Extract

¾ Cup Instant Coffee Granules

Instructions

Add 1 or 2 teaspoons, depending on the strength desired, to a cup of hot water and stir.

Day 7: I Believe In You

Today, I want you to know that I believe in you. To believe means to have confidence in, and I am fully confident that you have within you the ability to be who I made you to be, as well as the courage to accomplish all that is in your heart.

Sometimes it's hard for you to believe in yourself, to believe that you have what it takes for the journey. But My Child, you do not walk alone. You see, I created you with a unique purpose, a destiny that is yours and yours alone. There is no one on this earth that can accomplish what I created you to do. But you must put your confidence in Me, that I will do what I said I would do, and then you must have confidence in yourself, because with Me all things are possible!

Stay close to me, and listen for my direction. I will show you the path to take. Listen to the whispers of your heart. Those desires that burn so strong, I put them there. But you must wait for my perfect timing. Do not run ahead, but remain close by My side, and we will go together.

Do you dare to believe that you were created to do extraordinary things? Do not lose heart. I believe in you!

Reflection

What are some of the things that you believe God for in your life? Write them down. Ask God to give you the courage to dare to believe that with His help, you can accomplish all that is in your heart.

_____

_____

_____

_____

_____

_____

_____

_____

_____

Prayer

Father, thank You for believing in me. Thank You for the dreams, visions, and desires You've placed in my heart. Will You give me the courage to believe that with Your help I have what it takes to accomplish all that I desire to do? Thank You for never giving up on me.

Day 8: Tear Down Those Walls

Do you know that I am your Protector? Do you believe that I am for you, not against you? I see the walls again, the ones you put up in order to protect yourself from further hurt and pain. I know you've experienced disappointment, pain, and loss in your life, but I want to remind you that through all of it, I never left your side. When you cried in the darkness of the night and you felt as if no one understood, I was there. I caught every tear and placed it in a bottle.

Do you believe that I will turn your mourning into dancing? Do you believe that I desire to take your weeping and turn it into joy? I promise you, JOY truly does come in the morning. (Psalm 30:11)

If I am to fill you with the fullness of joy that you desire, you must first trust me enough to let your guard down. Can we begin to work together to tear down the walls that you have put over your heart? This protective barrier was good for a season, but I desire to bring you through the pain of your past into a future filled with peace, hope and joy.

I promise to be with you through the tearing down process. This, too, may be painful, but these walls will serve as monuments, places of remembrance in your life where you dared to allow yourself to feel joy once again. And don't worry; I am not breaking out the sledgehammer. We can chisel away together, slowly, carefully. Once the walls have come down, we can begin to rebuild and strengthen these places in your heart.

Remember, I am your strength. I am your Strong Tower. Run to me. I will keep you safe. I promise.

The name of the LORD is a strong tower; the righteous man runs into it and is safe.
(Proverbs 18:10)

Reflection

Do you feel you have put up walls in order to protect yourself from further hurt and pain? If so, take a moment and ask the Lord to reveal what happened to cause you to want to protect your heart.

_____

_____

_____

_____

_____

_____

_____

_____

_____

Prayer

Father, I admit that I have built walls around my heart to avoid further hurt and pain. I want to give You all of my heart, so that You will come and bring healing. Will You help me to remove the walls so that I can receive more of Your love? Thank you for the freedom that is only found in You, Jesus!

Coffee Brownies

Adapted from Pete Bakes

Ingredients

1 Cup Butter, Soft

2 Cups Sugar

2 Tsp Vanilla

4 Eggs

4 Oz Unsweetened Baking Chocolate, Melted And Cooled

1 Cup Flour

1/2 Cup Chocolate Chips

2-3 Tbsp Instant Coffee

Instructions

In a large bowl, blend together butter and sugar.

Add vanilla, eggs, melted chocolate, coffee, flour and chocolate chips.

Pour into a greased and floured 9×13 inch pan and bake at 325 degrees for 35 minutes.

Day 9: Let Me Wash Over You

My child, as you sit here this morning, I want you to allow My words of truth to wash over you. Now that we've removed the walls that you previously had kept up to protect your heart, allow My words to sink deep into the core of who you are.

You are chosen.

I chose you before the world was created. I desired to have a close and intimate relationship with you. I chose you to be My counterpart.
You were never meant to sit alone in a corner, watching the world go by. I chose you, and I have a plan and a purpose that is uniquely yours.
(Ephesians 1:5)

You are loved.

I came because I love you. I said "yes" to the will of My Father because you are worth it.
There is nothing that you could ever do to make me love you any less. I have been bound to you in love, forever.
(Romans 8:38-39)

You are beautiful.

*You captivate my heart with just one glance of your
eye. You are altogether lovely. You were created in
the image and likeness of My Father.
He is the essence of beauty.
(Song of Solomon 4:9)*

Having been washed in the water of My Word,
which is truth, you can leave this place today with
your head held high. You are my chosen bride. You
are loved and beautiful!

Reflection

Which of the above affirmations do you have the hardest time believing? Ask the Lord to help you to understand why you struggle to believe these things about yourself and write down what He speaks to your heart.

_____
_____
_____
_____
_____
_____
_____
_____
_____

Prayer

Father, I confess that I often have a hard time believing what Your Word says about me is true. Will You show me when these lies entered my life? Will You come and bring healing to my heart so that I can fully accept myself as you have accepted me? Thank you for affirming who I am in You.

Day 10: I Desire You

My daughter, I see you, standing there with your head bowed low, your eyes turned away in shame as you fear the false reality that you've built up within your walls. Do not turn your gaze from Me. Look deep into My eyes. For do you not know that I see you? I see the depth of your heart. I see your brokenness, the hurt and the pain, intermixed with the joys of life. I see dreams, buried underneath the rubble of "I should have", "I could have" and "if only". I see it all, for I am the God who sees you.

My beloved daughter, how you captivate Me when your glance meets Mine. Oh, that you would give Me your heart — your whole heart. I want that part that tries to remain hidden in the dark corners, those places where you have swept the crumbs of your life, afraid that I would not have them. I want that part of you. I long to take the broken pieces of your life and make you whole, My beloved. I long for you to feel My arms around you. I want you to experience My love in its fullness.

There is nothing that you can withhold from Me that I do not already know. Will you give Me your whole heart? Every empty place, everything that lies hidden in the dark places of your heart—even those places I desire. For even those places I desire. For you are My beloved, and My desire is for you!

I am my beloved's, and His desire is for me.
(Song of Solomon 7:10)

Reflection

Put on soft worship music and allow God to search your heart. Are there places that remain empty or unfulfilled that are in need of God's healing touch? Write them down.

_____

_____

_____

_____

_____

_____

_____

_____

_____

Prayer

Heavenly Father, today I surrender all of myself to You. I give You my whole heart, all the hurt, the pain, the empty places. I offer the pieces of my life to You today. Come and make me whole again. Thank you that You desire me, even in my brokenness.

Coffee Crunch Cake

*Darliene Johnson. Used with permission.

Ingredients

1 ¼ Cups Sifted Flour

¾ Cup Sugar

½ Cup Egg Yolks (8 and at room temperature)

¼ Cup Cold Water

1 Tablespoon Lemon Juice

1 Teaspoon Vanilla

1 Cup Egg Whites (8)

1 Teaspoon Salt

¾ Cup Sugar

Instructions

Sift flour and ¾ cup sugar into bowl. Make a well in center and add egg yolks, cold water, lemon juice and vanilla. Beat until it forms a thick, moderately smooth batter. Whip egg whites and salt until a very fine foam forms. Add ¾ cup sugar gradually, 2 tablespoons at a time. Continue beating until meringue is firm and holds up in straight peaks. Pour batter slowly over meringue while gently folding in with spoon. Fold in just until blended. Gently push batter into ungreased bundt pan. Break bubbles with knife.

Bake at 350 degrees for 50-55 minutes or until the top springs back lightly when touched. Immediately turn pan over, placing tub of pan over the neck of a bottle. Allow cake to hang until cold. Loosen and put cake on plate.

16-20 servings.

Coffee Crunch Topping

1 ½ Cups Sugar

¼ Cup Coffee Beverage

¼ Cup White Karo Syrup

3 Tablespoons Baking Soda (Sifted Before Measuring)

Stir to combine ingredients. Bring to a boil and cook to hard crack stage (310 degrees). Remove from heat and immediately add soda, which has been pressed through a sieve and measured lightly. Stir vigorously just until mixture thickens and pulls away from pan. Pour foamy mass into ungreased 9x9 pan. Do not destroy foam. Do not stir or spread. Let stand without moving until cool.

When ready to garnish cake, knock out of pan and crush between sheets of waxed paper with rolling pin to form coarse crumbs. To prepare Fiesta Cake, split cake into 4 equal layers. Have crunch ready.

Whipped Frosting

Place In Chilled Bowl:

2 Cups Whipping Cream (1 Pt.)

2 Tablespoons Sugar

2 Tablespoons Vanilla

Spread over cake, cover with crunch. Refrigerate until read to serve.

Day 11: I Will Hold You

My child, remember those times when you were afraid and you longed for your daddy's strong arms to hold you? Sometimes he did, but perhaps he was unable or unwilling to hold you the way you desired to be held. In those times, I want you to know that I was there.

When you were afraid,

I held you until My peace overwhelmed you.

When you felt alone,

I held you until you could feel My Holy Spirit within you.

When you were confused,

I held you until clarity took over your mind.

When you were angry,

I held you until the tears fell and you felt My love.

When you felt hopeless,

I held you until hope arose in your heart.

I didn't just hold you then. I hold you now. Can you feel My strong arms around you? Do you feel loved and at peace?

On those days where you long for your daddy's arms, reach up! I will pick you up and hold you. I will never let you go!

Reflection

Put on soft worship music and ask the Lord to come close. He promises that if we draw near to Him, He will draw near to us. Allow the Lord to show you a time in your life where He held you. Write it down and ask the Lord to speak to your heart about how He felt toward you in that moment.

_____

_____

_____

_____

_____

_____

_____

_____

_____

Prayer

Father, I confess that I long to be held, loved and accepted. Will You come and hold me now? Help me to feel Your warm, strong embrace. Speak to my heart about how You feel toward me at this moment. Thank you for allowing me to hear and feel Your heartbeat for me.

Day 12: You Are Loved

My child, believe Me when I tell you that I love you. Please don't turn away. I know it's hard for you to comprehend how I can love you so much. But this is not for you to figure out. You simply must trust. Trust in My love for you and know that I will never ever love you any less than I do now.

Allow Me to show you My love — the length, width, depth and height of My love. It is as vast as the ocean. It goes on forever. It will never end. I want you to rest and be secure in My love for you.

I love you,
no matter what.

I love you,
despite your failures.

I love you,
with all of your imperfections.

I love you,
beyond your sin and shame.

I love you,
even when you run from me.

I love you,
and I will never fail you.

I have loved you with an everlasting love.
(Jeremiah 31:3)

You do not have to do anything to earn My love. I simply want you to learn to sit with Me, talk with Me, and share your heart with Me. My love for you is patient and kind. Even when you turn away from Me, My love is relentless and will seek after you. Nothing will ever change the way that I feel about you. Rest in My love for you today.

Reflection

Write down the ways God reveals His love to you through His Word. What are some other ways that you see God demonstrating His love to you in the ordinary moments of each day?

_____

_____

_____

_____

_____

_____

_____

_____

_____

_____

Prayer

Lord, You are not just a God of love; You are love. The very essence of who You are is love. Will You help me to believe that You love me, just the way that I am? Thank you that nothing will ever separate me from Your love.

Coffee Pancakes

Adapted from A Cozy Kitchen

Ingredients

Yields 8 Small Pancakes

1 Cup Of All-Purpose Flour

1 Teaspoon Baking Powder

1 Teaspoon Baking Soda

1/2 Teaspoon Salt

1 1/2 Teaspoon Sugar

1 Egg

1 Cup Buttermilk

1 Tablespoon Instant Coffee Granules

Instructions

Pre-heat oven to 150˚F to keep pancakes warm while the others are cooking.

In a medium bowl, sift together flour, baking powder, baking soda, salt and sugar.

In a large measuring cup (or small bowl), beat together the egg and buttermilk.

Next, whisk in instant coffee until completely blended. In two batches, add the wet ingredients to the dry ingredients and mix until *just* combined.

The batter should have some small to medium lumps.

Heat griddle or cast iron skillet over medium low-heat and brush with 1 tablespoon butter. Using a 1/4 cup measure, add the batter to the warm skillet and cook until bubbles form along the sides and in the center. Flip. And cook on opposite side until golden brown.

Serve with warm maple syrup and a dollop of butter.

Day 13: You Are Good

My daughter, how are you feeling today? I hear that deep sigh as you shrug your shoulders. You don't have to use words to tell me that you aren't feeling too good about yourself right now. Somewhere along the way you've stopped believing that you are good, or that anything you do is good.

Let's look at some other words that describe "good": *virtuous, righteous, upright, moral, ethical, exemplary, irreproachable, blameless, guiltless, honorable, respectable, noble, trustworthy, praiseworthy, admirable; angelic.*

These are heavy words to take on. *Remember the labels?* They somehow wedge their way into your mind until you think about yourself as less than you are:

You don't feel like a good woman.

You don't believe you're a good wife.

You don't think you're a good mom.

You aren't sure you have anything good to offer to anyone.

Let Me bring you back to reality for a moment. Everything that I spoke into existence, everything that I created is good. After I fashioned you, I looked upon your beauty and said, "it is good".

You are a good woman,
because you strive to love Me with your whole heart.

You are a good wife,
because you seek to honor your husband and love him unconditionally.

You are a good mom,
because you love your children fiercely and desire to show them My love.

You, My beloved one, have so much good to offer to this world. You are good, because I am good, and My goodness lives in you.

Surely goodness and mercy shall follow me all the days of my life, and I shall dwell in the house of the Lord forever.
(Psalm 23:6)

Reflection

Everything that God created is good. That includes you. Take a moment to write down the qualities you see in yourself that are good. What are the qualities that others have seen in you that are good?

_____

_____

_____

_____

_____

_____

_____

_____

_____

Prayer

Lord, help me to see the goodness that is inside of me. Help me to cast off the lies that tell me I am not good, or that I have nothing to offer. Help me to believe that Your goodness lives in me, and therefore I am good. Thank you that Your goodness and mercy will follow me all the days of my life

.

Day 14: You Are Valued

Today I want to talk to you about value. Everything in this world has value of some kind. Not everything has a monetary value. For example, you value your time with Me, because you come away feeling strengthened and encouraged. You value your time with your family, because you are making memories. You value your time with friends because they lift you up when you are weak.

Do you know that you, My child, are of great value?

I know you don't often feel valuable. I know that you cannot imagine that you have anything of value to give to others. But please understand that you do not have to "give" anything to be of value. Remember that I love you, and that I paid a high price to purchase you back from darkness. Your worth and value far exceeds what your mind could comprehend.

The next time you feel invaluable, or as if you have nothing to give, remember that the weight of your worth and value is not determined by what you do. It is simply because of who you are, a daughter of the Most High King. You are My Child, and therein lies your value.

Reflection

Is it hard for you to understand the value that you have in Christ? Do you feel like you must do something to be of value to God, or someone else? As you meditate on God's Word, allow Him to show you your worth and value.

_____

_____

_____

_____

_____

_____

_____

_____

_____

Prayer

Father, I believe that You paid a high price for me when You took my sin and shame and died on the cross, just for me. Will You help me to see myself as valuable and that my value lies in You, and not in anything that I could do. Thank you that in Your eyes, Lord, I am valuable.

Coffee Toffee Bars

*Adapted from Tasty Kitchen

Ingredients

1 Cup Soft Butter Or Margarine

1 Cup Brown Sugar

1 Teaspoon Almond Extract

1 Tablespoon Instant Coffee (Up To 2 Tablespoons For More Flavor)

½ Teaspoon Baking Powder

¼ Teaspoon Salt

2-1/2 Cups Flour (Approx.)

1 Cup Chocolate Chips (Can Use Up To 2 Cups)

Instructions

Cream together butter and brown sugar.

Blend in almond extract, instant coffee, baking power and salt.

Add enough flour to make a stiff dough.

Press into a well-greased 9x13 pan and sprinkle chocolate chips on top.

Bake at 350 F for 20-25 minutes.

Day 15: You Are Not a Failure

My daughter, do you know how proud I am of you? I know that you do not always feel like you accomplish what you set out to do. I understand that you often feel as if you fall short and disappoint those you love. Believe Me when I say that this couldn't be farther from the truth.

I see your downcast eyes, and your heart that is broken in two. I see you striving to live up to expectations that you were never meant to live up to. You have a heart of gold — always willing to serve, always desiring to put others before yourself. But dear one, you were never meant to live up to such high standards.

Can I tell you something? You are NOT a failure! I see you. I see all that you do for those you love. I see all that you strive to do for Me, but I want you to cease from your striving. I want you to rest in My love and understand that you are enough. Your Father in heaven is most proud of His beautiful daughter. You are My girl, and you do not have to do anything to earn My love and affection.

Reflection

Think of a time when you felt like a failure. It can be a memory from the past, or a part of your life now. Ask the Lord to show you the lie that you believe about yourself that causes you to feel as if you cannot measure up.

_____

_____

_____

_____

_____

_____

_____

_____

_____

_____

Prayer

Lord, I confess that I have felt like a failure in this area of my life. Please forgive me for believing that I could do this in my own strength. Will You come and open my heart to receive the truth of Your Word for me in this area? I know that in my weakness You are made strong. Thank you, Lord, that in You all things are possible.

Day 16: You Are Equipped

My precious one, I see you standing inside the gate as you look out over all that lies ahead of you. Your heart yearns to move forward, to leave the safe place you've created within the routine and mundane. You yearn for the more, yet you hold back, as fear would tell you that you are not equipped for the journey. And here you remain, inside the gate, feeling stuck, bound, unable to move, fearing you don't have what it takes.

Do you hear Me calling you forth? I am beckoning you to come and see all that I've set out before you. Because I have called you, I will equip you. I would never call you to do something without first preparing you for the task. And most importantly, I promise to go with you. You will never accomplish anything without Me. Remember, My yoke is easy, My burden light. You need not fear failure. You will only fail if you don't try.

I have given you every resource for the journey.

For who is God, but the Lord? And who is a rock, except our God—the God who equipped me with strength and made my way blameless?

He made my feet like the feet of a deer
and set me secure on the heights.
(Psalm 18:31-33)

It's okay to step outside that gate now. Take My hand and let's begin the journey. Allow Me to show you all that your heart has been dreaming about, all that I've called you to do. I cannot promise you that it will always be easy. You may slip, you may take a wrong turn, but I will be right there to set your feet upon the right path once again. You will not fall. I promise that I will catch you.

There is maturing and growth that will only happen as you step out and give yourself permission to pursue what is in your heart. Unless you take the step forward, you will remain stagnant and unfulfilled. But move, and I go with you.

You are ready, My Daughter! Open the gate and run to where I am. You are equipped for the journey. And remember, the work that I started in you, I will complete. You need only say yes.

Reflection

Do you see yourself standing inside the gate, looking out at all that is ahead of you? Do you feel unprepared for the journey? Take a few moments to lay your fears before God. Write them down, and then use His Word to contradict those fears. Break off the lies that keep you where you are now. Remember, He will never leave you nor abandon you.

_____

_____

_____

_____

_____

_____

_____

_____

_____

_____

Prayer

Father, thank you that in You I have all that I need for the journey ahead. Will You help me to cling to You, to Your Word, and believe that You will bring me through to the other side? Thank you for giving me the opportunity to pursue all that You've placed in my heart. Give me the courage to step out!

Fajitas

*Adapted from Treebeards Cookbook

Ingredients

3 Skirt Steaks

6 Tablespoons Tomato Paste

1-1/4 Cups Brewed Strong Coffee

½ Cup Worcestershire Sauce

1 Tablespoon Sugar

2 Tablespoons Salt

2 Teaspoons Cayenne

1 Teaspoon Black Pepper

3 Tablespoons Freshly Squeezed Lime Juice

¼ Cup Vegetable Oil

Warm Flour Tortillas

Pico De Gallo

Sour Cream

Instructions

Trim skirt steak of all visible fat tough membrane. Set aside. Combine remaining marinade ingredients and mix well. Place meat in large zippered freezer bag and cover with marinade. Refrigerate overnight, turning meat several times.

Prepare grill until coals are white-hot. Grill steaks 6 minutes on each side or until meat reaches desired doneness.

Meanwhile, place marinade in large skillet; simmer while meat is cooking. When meat is done, slice into thin pieces.

To serve, spread warm tortilla with sour cream. Place a small amount of meat in center and top with pico de gallo. Drizzle with cooked marinade sauce, if desired. Roll up to eat!

Serves 6.

Day 17: You Are Beautiful

My daughter, I want you to hear Me when I tell you, "You are Beautiful". Don't turn away. Lift your eyes to Mine and listen to My heart for you. I understand that it is often hard for you to accept that you were created beautifully, in My very image. I know that there may have been events in your life that have caused you to believe otherwise. Your beauty has nothing to do with your past, your present or your future. The lie that would tell you that you are not beautiful, not desired, could not be farther from the truth!

Remember my love letter to you? What does it have to say about how beautiful you are?

Behold, you are beautiful, my love; behold, you are beautiful; your eyes are doves.
(Song of Solomon 1:15)

How beautiful and pleasant you are, O loved one, with all your delights!
(Song of Solomon 7:6)

My desire is that you would walk in the full understanding of how I see you. You captivate Me, every time I see you. I love to look at you! True beauty is not reflected by outward appearance, but rather by what is found on the inside. Learn to walk in love, joy, peace, patience, kindness, goodness, faithfulness, gentleness and self-control, and you will portray your beauty to others. Most importantly, My beauty will be reflected in you, and therefore you will become all the more beautiful.

Even in your imperfections and unfinished state, you are still beautiful! Be patient, My love, I am not finished with you yet!

Reflection

Do you feel beautiful? If not, ask the Lord to reveal the hurt and pain that has caused you to not believe this truth. Ask Him to help you to remove the lies that you have believed about yourself and replace them with the truth of His Word.

Prayer

Father, I want to believe You when You tell me that I am beautiful. Will You help me? Remind me of the words that You speak over me, and allow them to sink deep into my heart. Help me to see myself as You see me, beautiful and desired. Thank you, Lord, that I am Your masterpiece, perfectly formed in Your hand.

Day 18: You Are Forgiven

My child, I see your heart is heavy this morning as your mind is racing with thoughts of, *"Why didn't I, how could I have, and what will people think?"* Your shoulders fall under the weight of these thoughts that your mind refuses to let go of.

"You should have done better."

"You should not have said anything."

"You should have run the other way."

"Why did you do it?"

I want to remind you this morning that the heaviness that you carry is not yours to keep. These feelings of guilt and shame were taken with Me to the cross. I paid the price. For all of it. For every wrong move, selfish motive, and hasty decision. For every unclean thought, impure motive and misguided judgment. It was all nailed to the cross, as I held them in the palm of My hand, refusing to let go, refusing to let you go.

The next time you feel guilt and shame, will you remember that I took it all. Will you remember My nail-scarred hands, and the blood that was shed? It was all for you. You no longer need to feel ashamed. You no longer need to listen to those negative thoughts that tell you that you are no good, unclean or impure. You need only remember that you are Mine and that I bought you back with a price.

You are My redeemed one.

You are pure and spotless in My eyes.

You are forgiven.

My daughter, you are forgiven and free, for all eternity.

Reflection

Take a moment to list examples from God's Word where He makes himself known as the Reedemer. Do you believe that God has fully forgiven you and has redeemed you from your past?

_____

_____

_____

_____

_____

_____

_____

_____

_____

Prayer

Father, thank you for not only forgiving my sin, but for redeeming me and making me new. Help me to understand what it means to be redeemed, fully pardoned for all of my sin. Thank You, Jesus, for dying on the cross for me so that I could have a new life, and live eternally with You.

*Denise In Bloom. Used with permission.

Ingredients

1 ½ Cups Instant Coffee Granules

1 ½ Cups Hot Chocolate Mix

2 Cups Powdered Non-Dairy Creamer

1 ½ Cups Sugar

½ Teaspoon Ground Nutmeg

1 ½ Teaspoons Ground Cinnamon

Instructions

Mix 2 or 3 teaspoons in a cup or mug of hot water and stir for delicious coffee.

Day 19: You Are Free

Remember, My child, that you are free. I have broken the chains that once held you captive. Yet, sometimes you feel like you must hold back, as you feel unworthy to walk forward, not good enough for the task at hand. I want you to allow My Words to wash over you as your mind is once again renewed to these truths:

You are no longer in bondage to sin.

*For freedom Christ has set us free; stand firm
therefore, and do not submit again
to a yoke of slavery.
(Galatians 5:1)*

My truth has set you free.

*And you will know the truth,
and the truth will set you free.
(John 8:32)*

I have delivered you. I will keep you safe.

*Many are saying of my soul, there is no salvation
for him in God. Selah But you, O Lord, are a shield
about me, my glory, and the lifter of my head.*

Salvation belongs to the Lord; your blessing be on your people!
(Psalm 3:2-3, 8)

Your heart praises me, because you are free.

Bring me out of prison, that I may give thanks to your name! The righteous will surround me, for you will deal bountifully with me.
(Psalm 142:7)

I have rescued you because you love Me.

Because he holds fast to me in love, I will deliver him; I will protect him, because he knows my name. When he calls to me, I will answer him;
I will be with him in trouble;
I will rescue him and honor him.
(Psalm 91:14-15)

I have saved you from death.

For you have delivered my soul from death, yes, my feet from falling, that I may walk
before God in the light of life.
(Psalm 56:13)

You are free, because I have set you free. You are no longer bound to guilt and shame, no longer a prisoner of your past. You are not a slave, but My daughter, in whom I take great delight.

Reflection

Take a moment to remember all that God has freed you from. Write it down. This is your testimony, your very own history in God. Allow God to use your testimony to help bring others to Him.

_____

_____

_____

_____

_____

_____

_____

_____

Prayer

Father, thank You for the freedom that is in Christ Jesus. Thank You that my chains are gone and I have been set free to love You. Help me to walk out this freedom, to never take it for granted. Will You help me to remember the testimony of what Jesus did for me and to share Your love with others?

Day 20: Quiet Your Heart

Your heart is racing right now. I can feel it, beating fast. I can sense its yearnings. You long for stillness, for quiet, for peace in the midst of the chaos that surrounds you. As you sit here, longing to breathe Me in, you ache.

Although the process of stripping away all that lays heavily on your heart can take some time, I can show you how to quiet your heart so that you can once again be filled to overflowing. This does not necessarily mean that the noise all around you will be silenced, nor does it mean that the storm that is threatening to invade will not land directly in the middle of your space. I cannot promise you that the chaos you are experiencing in this moment won't be there in the morning.

The response of your heart in your quest for quiet should be to look at Me. Fix your eyes on Me, and get your eyes off of what you can see. When you purpose in your heart to look at Me and to trust Me, your heart will be filled with peace. Even in the midst of all that surrounds you, there is peace and quiet, but you must look at Me.

When you hear the noise and see the storm that looms, look up, My Child! Look into My eyes. There you will find the peace and quiet that your heart desires.

You keep him in perfect peace whose mind is stayed on you, because he trusts in you.
(Isaiah 26:3)

Reflection

What prevents you from quieting your heart before the Lord? What is it that competes for your daily quiet time with Jesus? Take a moment to write down the reasons why you sometimes struggle in this area.

_____

_____

_____

_____

_____

_____

_____

_____

_____

Prayer

Father, I desire to have a quiet and still heart before You. Will You help me to lay down my busyness and striving? Help me to unclutter my thoughts and clean out the places in my heart where I've allowed other things to fill. Empty me, Lord, so that I can be filled once again to overflowing with You.

Frappuccino Protein Shake

*Psycowith6. Used with permission.

Ingredients

1 Banana

1 Scoop Chocolate Protein Powder

1 Heaping Teaspoon Instant Coffee

10 Oz. Milk

10 Ice Cubes

Whip Cream (Optional)

Caramel Syrup (Optional)

Use the ice mode on your blender until smooth. Add whip cream and a drizzle of caramel syrup if desired.

Day 21: I Hear You

There you are. I see you, peering around the corner, longing for someone to talk to. Do you mind if I come and sit next to you? Can you feel My heart beating? It beats for you. Do you understand how much I adore you?

What's on your mind today, My child? Do you trust Me enough to pour your heart out to Me? Yes, I already know those issues that lie deep within, but I want you to release them to Me. Unless you empty yourself of the worries and cares in your heart, you will not be able to move forward.

I want you to know that I hear you. Every word spoken. Every word left unspoken. Every thought formed in your mind and every stirring of your heart. I hear you!

You are safe with Me, My child. You long to share your heart raw and exposed. Go ahead and empty yourself. I will not turn away my ear.

Incline your ear, O Lord, and answer me, for I am poor and needy. Preserve my life, for I am godly; save your servant, who trusts in you—you are my God. Be gracious to me, O Lord, for to you do I cry all the day. Gladden the soul of your servant, for to you, O Lord, do I lift up my soul. For you, O Lord, are good and forgiving, abounding in steadfast love to

all who call upon you. Give ear, O Lord, to my prayer; listen to my plea for grace. In the day of my trouble I call upon you, for you answer me.
(Psalm 86:1-7)

Reflection

Put on soft worship music. Invite God to come closer as you quiet your heart before Him. Now, share your heart with God, raw and exposed. Just pour yourself out without even thinking about what you are saying. Believe that He hears you!

_____

_____

_____

_____

_____

_____

_____

_____

_____

Prayer

Father, I confess that I often feel misunderstood or unheard. I believe that You incline Your ear to my every prayer. My heart is filled with gratitude just knowing You hear and understand the deep yearnings of my heart. Thank you, Lord, that you hear me.

Day 22: I Delight in You!

Do you remember as a little girl how you would dance and twirl, longing for someone to pay attention to you? You longed to be cherished, treasured in the eyes of those whom you loved. I know there were often times when you felt unloved, uncared for, uncherished. You worked so hard to be seen, to be forever imprinted in the eyes of those whom you loved.

Can I tell you something? I cherished you then, and I cherish you now.

I take great delight in you. You bring Me so much joy, and you don't have to do anything. My delight is in you, simply for who you are.

You are My child.
You are My daughter.
You are My princess.
You are My beloved one.
You are My bride.

You captivate me when you glance My way, if even for a moment. I cannot take My eyes off of you. I want you to know today how much joy you bring to My heart. I will forever cherish you, simply because you are worth being cherished.

*The Lord your God is in your midst, a mighty one
who will save; he will rejoice over you with
gladness; he will quiet you by his love; he will exult
over you with loud singing.
(Zephaniah 3:17)*

Reflection

Look up the word "delight" in the dictionary. Do you believe that you have to do something to earn the Lord's favor? Write down all that you feel you have to do to please Him. Next, write down all of the ways that God shows you He delights in you through His Word.

_____

_____

_____

_____

_____

_____

_____

_____

_____

_____

Prayer

Father, I confess that I feel like I must do something to earn Your approval, delight and pleasure. Will You help me to understand that You already delight in me, simply for who I am, not for what I do? Thank You, Lord, for loving and approving of me.

Tangy Coffee Barbeque Sauce

*Adapted from Today's Creative Blog

Ingredients

1 Cup Ketchup

1 Cup Dunkin' Donuts Brewed Coffee

2 Tablespoons Dark Brown Sugar

1 Tablespoon Dried Onion Flakes

1 Teaspoon Garlic Powder

1 Teaspoon Chili Powder

1 1/2 Teaspoon White Pepper

1 1/2 Tablespoons Balsamic Vinegar

1 1/2 Teaspoon Soy Sauce

Instructions

Combine ketchup, coffee, brown sugar, onion flakes, garlic powder and chili powder in a small saucepan; bring to a boil. Reduce heat and simmer 10 minutes or until slightly thickened, stirring occasionally. Remove from heat; stir in pepper, balsamic vinegar and soy sauce.

Day 23: I Will Carry You

Beloved, I cannot promise you that your journey will always be an easy one. But I can promise you that I will never leave you alone. I promise to be with you every step of the way, and I will bring you through it.

When you feel overwhelmed,

remember to take My yoke upon you, for My burden is light.

When you cannot see the road ahead,

remember to look up to the hills, for there your help will be.

When you cannot hear clearly,

remember to lean into My voice of wisdom and I will guide you.

When you feel like you can't go on,

surrender it all into My hands and let me carry you.

On those days when you feel overwhelmed, lean into Me and trust Me. Surrender it all into My hands and allow Me to carry you until you have the strength to walk again.

93

Reflection

Ask the Lord to show you all of the things in your life that you try to do on your own. Write them down. Now ask the Lord to come and lift you up and carry you off, away from those things that weigh you down. How does it make you feel to know that the Lord carries you when you do not have the strength to walk the journey on your own?

Prayer

Father, I confess that I get tired and weary at times and try to walk in my own strength. Will You help me to understand that it's okay to admit my weakness to You, knowing that You will carry me until I have the strength again? Thank You, Lord, that when I feel heavy and have not the strength to walk, You come and carry me through to the other side.

Day 24 – You Are an Overcomer

My daughter, you are an overcomer. You have the ability to overcome every obstacle and hardship in your life, because My strength is in you. I have overcome the world therefore you have the power to overcome.

I have told you these things, so that in me you may have peace. In this world you will have trouble. But take heart! I have overcome the world.
(John 16:33)

When the storms rage around you, you need only be still and wait for Me. I will fight for you! In Me, you are victorious. I know sometimes it seems like you are fighting an uphill battle, and victory is nowhere in sight. But I promise you that I am right there with you in the trenches and I will not abandon you.

With every step you take, you are gaining ground and getting closer to winning the race. Sometimes it will be one step forward and two steps back, but if you continue to move forward, you will cross the finish line. Do not allow the enemy to keep you from running the race that I have set out before you. Fix your gaze on Me, for I am the prize!

*I press on toward the goal for the prize of the
upward call of God in Christ Jesus.
(Phil. 3:14)*

When you find yourself struggling to run, to gain
the victory, remind yourself that I am for you, not
against you. Stand on the truth of My Word. I have
overcome the world and therefore, you will
overcome by My strength, which is in you.

Reflection

Are there things in your life that you have been fighting to overcome? Write them down. Picture yourself running hard and fast toward your goal. Do not look back. Do not grow weary. God will strengthen you.

_____

_____

_____

_____

_____

_____

_____

_____

_____

Prayer

Father, thank You for giving me the ability to overcome every obstacle that I face. Thank You that Your power in me helps me to run the race. I want to run hard after You, without looking back. Help me to fix my eyes on You Jesus, for You are the author and perfector of my faith. In You, I have the power to overcome!

The Weidner Steak Marinade

*Adapted from Tasty Kitchen

Ingredients

3 Tablespoons Extra Virgin Olive Oil

2 Tablespoons Soy Sauce

2 Tablespoons Worcestershire Sauce

2 Tablespoons Honey

2 Tablespoons Dijon Mustard

2 Tablespoons Freshly Minced Ginger

3 cloves Garlic, minced

1 pinch Crushed Red Pepper

½ teaspoon Coffee Grounds

Instructions

In small bowl, whisk ingredients together.

Place steaks into a Ziploc bag and pour the marinade into the bag.

Seal and place in fridge for at least 2 hours and up to 24 hours.

Grill steaks on medium high to desired doneness.

Serve with your favorite side dish.

Day 25: Come and Dance

My Daughter, I see you there, in the distance. Fear and darkness surround you. I hear your thoughts, *"What will I become if I give myself fully to Him?"* At times you prefer to tuck yourself away in the darkness, yet there is a light, My light, which beckons you to come. When you fully give in, fully surrender, you rise from the darkness and join Me.

I am calling you to come and dance with Me. My light swirling around you is inviting. Can you see the colors, many of which you've never seen before? They are drawing you in.

The child inside of you screams to get out. You want to run straight into the light, straight into My arms. There is no fear there, only childlike faith.

Will you come as that child? Will you let your guard down? Will you allow yourself to push through this darkness towards the place in the distance that draws you? It is not so far away. It is but a step. It is but the willingness of your heart. You will overcome this fear. Push through the darkness and join the One whose face you cannot see, but whose light captivates you.

Step out in faith, My daughter. Trust Me. Come and dance with the One who calls You by name.

Reflection

Put on soft worship music, and picture yourself dancing with Jesus. How does it make you feel? Write down all of the things that you feel get in the way of fully and completely trusting Jesus. Imagine yourself running into His arms, with reckless abandon and surrender.

_____

_____

_____

_____

_____

_____

_____

_____

_____

Prayer

Lord, thank You that You desire to partner with me in this dance of life. Will You help me to trust You Lord? Help me to surrender my life completely to You. I believe that You will always guide and lead me well. Thank You, Lord, that I can come to You as a child, and that You desire to dance with me. Help me to sense Your nearness today.

Day 26: You Are a Song

My daughter, YOU are a song! It doesn't matter if you feel like you sing well or not. It's not about making a melody or harmony, with perfect pitch. But it's about allowing yourself to be the YOU that I created YOU to be.

There has been a song placed in your heart from the time you were created. I have given you a unique voice, beautiful to My ear, and one that resounds as a crescendo up to heaven. Your voice desires to be heard, to bring glory and honor to My name.

{Oh, I can hear you humming along now!}

Only YOU can sing the song that I put in YOU! Open your mouth, dear one. Open your heart, beloved one. Open your soul and spirit and breathe in deep and allow that heavenly sound to arise.

I am waiting to hear your voice! Your song is meant to be sung for all of the world to hear!

Reflection

When you think of being a song for the Lord, what kind of song would you be? God has gifted you with a voice like no other. Take a few moments to write down how God is using your voice today to bring Him glory.

_____

_____

_____

_____

_____

_____

_____

_____

_____

_____

Prayer

Lord, thank You that You have gifted me with a voice. Help me to be obedient to use my voice, first to praise You, and next to build others up. Will You come and put the melody and harmony in my heart that You desire to be sung? Thank You for the privilege of allowing my voice to be heard. It's all for Your glory, Lord.

Pumpkin Spice Latte Poke Cake

*Adapted from Cooking Mimi

Ingredients

1 Two Layer Sized Yellow Cake Mix

1 15 Ounce Can Pure Pumpkin

3 Eggs

1/3 Cup Oil

1 Cup Water

1 Teaspoon Instant Coffee Granules

1 Tablespoon Pumpkin Pie Spice

1 14 Ounce Can Sweetened Condensed Milk

1/2 Cup Half And Half Or Whole Milk

1 8 Ounce Tub Whipped Topping, Thawed

Instructions

Spray a 9 by 13 inch pan with cooking spray. Preheat oven to 350 degrees.

Combine cake mix, pumpkin, eggs, oil, water, coffee granules, and pumpkin pie spice in a large bowl or bowl of a stand mixer. Beat on medium speed for 2 minutes. Pour into prepared pan and bake at 350 degrees for 25-30 minutes or until a tester comes out with fine crumbs.

In a small bowl combine sweetened condensed milk and half and half.

When cooled to room temperature poke holes in the cake using the handle of a wooden spoon. Pour the sweetened condensed milk and half and half over cake. Refrigerate for several hours or overnight. If the milk pools in the corners of the pan as it chills spoon it over the top.

When ready to serve spread the whipped topping over the cake and sprinkle individual servings with cinnamon or pumpkin pie spice.

Day 27: You Were Made to Love

My daughter, I created you to love others. When your heart is filled with My love, you will learn how to love. I know you often feel as if you are unable to love. In and of yourself, you cannot love. It takes My love in you to be able love, fully and completely. Just like I give you the ability to love Me, so I will give you the ability to love others.

When you pour your heart out to Me and fall in love with Me, I will show you how to love. When you learn to abide in Me, to remain in a place of communion with Me, I will give you the ability to love out of the overflow.

"Abide in me, and I in you. As the branch cannot
bear fruit by itself, unless it abides in the vine,
neither can you, unless you abide in me. .
This is my commandment, that you love one
another as I have loved you.
(John 15:4, 12)

You were created to love. So go on, love deeply. Love fiercely. Love without reservation. Love without expecting anything in return. Take My hand, and let Me show you how to love.

Reflection

Read John 15. How has Jesus called us to love Him? How are we called to love others? Write down several examples in God's Word where He shows you His love for you, and for others.

Prayer

Father, help me to abide in You. Give me a desire for Your Word and for Your presence. Help me to cling to You with every breath, every fiber of my being. Will You fill me up with Your love, and allow that love to overflow into the lives of those around me? Thank you, Lord, for filling me to overflowing with Your love so that I can give it away to others.

Day 28: You Were Made to Shine

Do you know that My glory resides in you? It's time to let it out!

You were called to be a beacon of light for all the world to see. You may not think that you have much light to give. Do not let the word "glory" make you shrink back. There is a time for glory to be displayed in miracles, signs and wonders. But did you know that My glory is sometimes better displayed through the simplicity of just loving Me and doing what it is I've created you to do? For what is glory but honor? What is glory but magnificence and beauty? What is glory but praise and thanksgiving?

You display My glory when you Honor Me and tell of My good works.

You display My glory when you seek Me and the beauty and majesty of My presence.

You display My glory when you praise Me and offer up thanksgiving.

My glory is already within you. It comes from that place of deeply abiding in Me.

I have called you to shine! So rise up, My love, My fair one, and shine forth.

Arise, shine, for your light has come, and the glory of the LORD has risen upon you.
(Isaiah 60:1)

Reflection

Where do you see God's glory around you? What are some of the ways that God's glory is displayed through you? What are the deepest desires of your heart?

_____

_____

_____

_____

_____

_____

_____

_____

_____

Prayer

Lord, let the light of Your face shine upon me. Everywhere I go, Lord, may Your glory be displayed. Thank You, Lord, that Your glorious light shines through me.

The Moistest, Yummiest, Most Delicious Chocolate Cake

*Adapted from Tasty Kitchen

Ingredients

2 Cups Sugar

1 – ¾ Cup Flour

1 – ½ Teaspoon Baking Powder

¾ Cups Baking Cocoa (Dutch Process Or Dark Chocolate If You Prefer Darker Taste)

1 – ½ Teaspoon Baking Soda

1 Teaspoon Salt

2 Whole Eggs

1 Cup Milk

½ Cups Vegetable Oil

2 Teaspoons Vanilla Extract

¾ Cups Hot, Strong Brewed Coffee (may need up to an additional ¼ Cup)

Instructions

Heat over to 350 F

Grease and flour two 9-inch round baking pans or one 13x9 inch pan.

In larger mixing bowl, stir together dry ingredients.

Add eggs, milk, oil and vanilla; beat on medium speed for 2 minutes

Stir in coffee by hand (batter will be thin). (*Start with a full cup of coffee. If you live in an exceptionally moist climate, 3.4 cup may be enough.)

Pour in prepared pan.

Bake for 30-35 minutes for round 9-inch pans, or 35-40 minutes for 9x13 pan or until center comes out clean. (*Do not use 8-inch pans or the batter will overflow. If you are using glass, allow for a little extra time.)

Cool for 10 minutes; remove pan from wire racks. Frost as desired.

Day 29: Go Ahead and Dream

Did you know that you were a dream in the heart of My Father before the beginning of time? He dreamt of you. Yes, you! His thoughts were always toward you, even before your existence. He fashioned you perfectly, uniquely, with a purpose. You are God's dream fulfilled!

It's okay to dream. I know your heart is fragile. I understand the pain and hurt that lies buried within you — lost hope and dreams yet unfulfilled. But I never want you to stop pursuing your dreams. Trust Me for the timing. Just because there are desires in your heart not yet realized, this does not mean that I am saying no. My timing is perfect.

I want you to keep pursuing those dreams. Never let them go. You might be asked to surrender them into my Hands for a season, or perhaps for eternity. One dream fully surrendered may mean the fulfillment of a greater dream, one put in your heart by My Father that you have not yet uncovered.

Go ahead and dream! My Father dreamt of you, and look what happened!

Reflection

What are some of the dreams that are in your heart? Go ahead, write them down, and begin to dream again.

_____

_____

_____

_____

_____

_____

_____

_____

_____

Prayer

Father, I confess that I have not taken the time to dream with You. Will You awaken the dreams that You have placed in my heart? Give me the wisdom and strength to believe that my dreams can come true. Thank You, Lord, for allowing me to dream and for reminding me that nothing is impossible with You.

Day 30: You Were Made for Greatness

You were made for greatness. I know most days you feel far from great, as life passes you by and all that you do feels mediocre, at best. Do not confuse greatness with perfection. I never called you to be perfect. To be great means to be above the normal, beyond average.

You are not called to be a bystander as life simply happens around you. No! I want you as an active and involved player on My team. I am calling you up, calling you to a higher standard. It's time for My greatness to shine forth in and through you.

The level of greatness that I am calling you to is this: I want you to be the best you that you can be. There is not another person on this earth that can do what it is I've called you to do.

Whatever it is you put your hands to,
do it excellently.
Whoever it is that you love,
love them deeply, fiercely.
Wherever you go, walk confidently.
Whenever you speak, tell of Me and My works.

The next time you feel ordinary, know that you are anything but ordinary. You are extraordinary in the eyes of a great and mighty God. A God who desires to share His greatness with you, so that you will be great in all that you do!

Reflection

How is God using the ways you feel small for big things today? Take a moment to dream. If you could do anything for God, what would that be?

_____

_____

_____

_____

_____

_____

_____

_____

Prayer

Father, You are great and most worthy of praise. I confess that I can do nothing apart from You. Help me to believe that You desire to do great things in and through me. Thank You, Lord, for the gifts and talents that You have given me. Help me to use them for Your glory, as You make Yourself even greater in and through me.

Vanilla Coffee Creamer

*Marathon Mom. Used with permission.

Ingredients

1 cup heavy cream (or 1/2 cup milk and 1/2 cup cream)

2 Tablespoons maple syrup

2 teaspoons vanilla extract

Instructions

Stir maple syrup and vanilla extract into cream (or cream/milk mixture).

In small saucepan over medium heat, stir mixture for just a couple minutes without bringing to boil. You need just enough heat to mingle the flavors together.

Stir into your favorite coffee while warm.

Store in refrigerator.

Day 31: Return to Me and Rest

Return to Me, My child. I see you in your striving. You move from room to room, from place to place, from task to task seeking perfection. You labor, all good things, yet how soon you forget that it's a partnership, you and Me. For apart from Me, you can do no good thing. Will you come to Me again, My child, and allow Me to lift the shame, the guilt, the need to please, the desire to be perfect off your shoulders?

I have come to offer you My rest, yet instead you say, *"just a moment"* or *"when I'm done with this one last thing."* And the rest never comes. Oh, you may sit for a bit, but your mind is racing and your heart is broken at the failures you see in yourself every day. Your heart will never truly be at rest until you cease from your striving, lay down your selfish ways, and realize that you are in need of Me.

I want you to learn to cultivate a heart of stillness, to posture yourself at My feet, and to listen to my instruction. For My law is there for Your good. *Will you come and allow Me to enlighten My Word in your heart?* I want you to learn to live a life from the overflow, overflowing with My goodness and grace, but you cannot do that unless you learn to be still, to sit and ponder My Words in your heart.

It's only when you come in your weakness and brokenness and admit that you need Me that you will find Me. There is nothing that you can do alone that will give you the strength and confidence to accomplish all that you have on your plate each day. I know that you are feeling weak and weary, but remember that My power is perfected in your weakness. I would much rather have you in your weakened and humbled state, than full of pride and arrogance. It's through a weak and humble heart that I work best.

My child, never forget My love for you. Even during those times when you choose to turn away from Me, My love still seeks after you. I will never leave you and I will never forsake you. But how much easier would your life be if you would only enter into partnership with Me from the rising of the sun through its setting?

"In returning and rest you shall be saved; in quietness and in trust shall be your strength."
(Isaiah 30:15)

Come, My child, and return to Me and rest.

Reflection

Ask Jesus to show you all the things in your life that are distracting you and keeping you from His presence. Write them down. Ask Him to help you to make a schedule and show you how to bring balance to your life.

_____

_____

_____

_____

_____

_____

_____

_____

_____

_____

Prayer

Father, forgive me for allowing other things, people and ministry to keep me from a deeper relationship with You. Today I say, "Yes," to Your will and to Your way, Lord. Help me to put You first, before all other things, that I may walk in the fullness of all that You have for me, with joy.

About the Author

Barbie lives in Northern California with her husband of 25 years. Together they have four beautiful children and a son-in-love. She works full time at Convergence House of Prayer in Fremont, CA, assisting her Pastor and the Children's Equipping Center. She loves to worship, paint, and encourage the hearts of women.

Barbie blogs at MyFreshlyBrewedLife.com, where she offers glimpses of His love and sprinkles of His grace for every day living.

Made in the USA
Las Vegas, NV
03 January 2021

15253326R00074

Are you ready to draw closer to Jesus?

31 days of devotionals and coffee-infused recipes

The way that you develop any relationship is to be a good listener and to spend time with the other person. *Coffee Talk With Jesus* is a compilation of intimate letters from the heart of God for His daughters. As you read this 31-day devotional, may your heart be awakened to how much your Heavenly Father loves and accepts you.

In Christ,

Barbie Swihart

M y F r e s h l y B r e w e d L i f e . c o

ISBN 9781494216887

9000

9 781494 216887